Jo Cauldrick

The
WITCH'S
HOME

RITUALS AND CRAFTS FOR
PROTECTION AND HARMONY

Hardie Grant

BOOKS

CONTENTS

INTRODUCTION

*F*or as long as I can remember, I have been a craft-loving, creative soul. The love of nature and crafting has never left me. My grandmother taught me so much about garden magic and the moon, my mum about crafting and being a free spirit. After having my children, I began to research deeper spiritual practices, which led to the birth of my business The Moon Journal back in 2017.

There's not a day that goes by that I'm not dreaming about making something or actually making something, whether that's in my garden or in my apartment. The act of creating something with my hands holds so much magic and potential.

Now, with the resurgence of mysticism and natural witchcraft, so many more people are enriching their lives by using the powerful properties of herbs, plants, flowers and crystals. The cycles of the seasons and the moon are being used to find rhythm and self-reflection, and spiritual practices are helping us to navigate our experiences. The home is becoming a place that reflects and amplifies magic.

When we care for our homes, we also care for ourselves. Self-care is about honouring your time and energy, it's about setting healthy boundaries and feeling worthy of having a life that not only feels authentic to you but builds on the magic you already have within you.

ABOUT THIS BOOK

*I*mmerse yourself in the world of magical crafts that will bring inspiration, relaxation and harmony to your home and enhance your spiritual practice.

Your home is unique to you, it's where you should feel safe, secure, happy, loved and free to express your creativity.

I believe that the home is sentient and holds her own energy, memories and desires. The home works with reciprocal energy that is flowing all the time. If you're feeling in a rut, unhappy or just need to shake the energy up, the chances are that your home is holding those negative energies.

This book will give you practical crafting activities and rituals that can shift that energy and attract abundance into your home and life. You're not aiming for an Instagrammable house, you're aiming to create sacred spaces that help you feel fresh, cosy, inspired and content.

I also share my love of altar spaces. An altar space refers to a small area in your home that has a spiritual and often seasonal focus. It's a place to display crystals, oracle cards and natural objects that have meaning. Your altar space is sacred and cherished, it is a place of inspiration and introspection.

Sometimes, you just need a spark of inspiration and the confidence to live your most authentic life – and what better place to start than where your heart is: your home.

THE CONCEPT OF SELF-CARE

Self-care is a term used to describe the importance of treating yourself with compassion. It is a holistic philosophy that invites you to become more aware of your physical, emotional and spiritual needs.

Often in our hectic, production-obsessed society, we can feel burnt out and drained, and this is because of a lack of self-care. Self-care practices can uplift, nurture, nourish, inspire and heal you.

Self-care is about walking your own magical path, creating rhythms and rituals in tune with the moon and nature and that honour your home space. It nudges you to set healthy boundaries with your time and energy and to find deeper meaning in your life. It's about knowing when to take action and when to rest.

A happy magical home is a happier more magical you.

𝒫ROTECTION

When you have a secure base to call your own, you feel safer and calmer. You are also responsible for the physical safety of your home, and the items within it. No matter how small or how large your home is, it should be treated with care and respect and with a sense of gratitude.

Protection isn't just a physical concept, there is always going to be a metaphysical component. In this chapter, I have included some practical and effective activities that will create a strong sense of harmony within your home.

HERBS FOR THE HOME

Herbs have been used for thousands of years to heal the mind, body and soul. Growing up, I spent many, many summers with my grandmother, who taught me all about the folklore associated with herbs and particularly where to place them in and around the home.

Herbs have powerful associations with healing, not only because of their incredible medicinal qualities, which are used in a plethora of modern-day medicines, but also because of their psychic and sensorial properties.

In astrology, each herb has a ruling planet and sacred element. The sacred elements are Air, Fire, Water and Earth. In Wiccan traditions they also include Spirit as the fifth sacred element.

This means that, based on the season and where you are in the world, each plant has an astrological link. The associations are made based on the shape of the blossoms, its distinguishing features, such as the colour of its petals, the location/environment it's found in and its traditional and folklore uses. For example, for a plant like the sunflower, which naturally tracks the sun, its ruling planet is the sun (in astrology, the sun and the moon are referred to as planets, even though they technically aren't).

Plants, herbs, flowers and trees have natural and magical properties that are amplified by their ruling planet. If you want to increase confidence and creativity, you may choose to conduct a spell on a Sunday (Sun Day) using the corresponding herbs. You can use herb essential oils in a diffuser, or cook with edible plant and herb varieties.

Rosemary

This is the good-neighbour herb when it's grown around your boundary or front gate; it amplifies harmonious energy between you and your neighbour. Because it is also such a great culinary herb, it's lovely to offer your neighbour a sprig of rosemary. It's a must-have for every home and garden and can be hung up to dry in your kitchen or near your altar space.

Basil

This is also known as the witch's herb. It's associated with fire and can be used in so many dishes to create a wonderful aromatic flavour. You can also use it to help attract healthy finances by adding a dried basil leaf to your wallet.

Lavender

This herb has one of the most recognisable scents. Bees and butterflies love it, and you instinctively want to run your hands through it whenever you walk past some. The colour purple is very harmonious; dried lavender looks beautiful and can be added to any cleansing wand because it smokes so well.

Here are some helpful plant/herb/flower associations. I've included three for each ruling planet, but there are many more.

Sun:
amplifies self-confidence and creativity

* Sunflower
* St John's wort
* Chamomile

Mercury:
aids clarity of thought and communication

* Cinnamon
* Lavender
* Thyme

Moon:
develops the subconscious mind and intuition

* Anise
* Cabbage
* Mugwort

Jupiter:
develops material success and ambition

* Cedar
* Saffron
* Dandelion

Mars:
amplifies motivational energy and passion

* Nettles
* Cumin
* Garlic

Venus:
amplifies artistic flare and beauty

* Myrtle
* Catnip
* Tansy

Saturn:
aids knowledge acquisition and protection
* Patchouli
* Rosemary
* St John's wort

Pluto:
corresponds to karmic cycles and transformation
* Mushrooms
* Myrrh
* Patchouli

Neptune:
develops imagination and manifesting
* Lotus
* Willow
* Poppy

Uranus:
aids self-development and breaking habits
* Allspice
* Clove
* Coffee

CRYSTALS FOR THE HOME

No magical home would be complete without the addition of crystals. Crystals hold memory and have their own unique makeup. Crystals can be used to relax, heal, inspire, protect and attract energy.

Crystals hold so much enchantment and power for those who use them. They are steeped in mystery, and many practitioners use them for healing.

Placing crystals and precious stones around your home inspires a sense of peace and tranquillity. The ancient Chinese tradition of feng shui uses a method of carefully considering where furniture and objects are placed. When placed well, it is thought that you and your environment become harmonised with the yin and yang energy. This is the same for crystals and their placement around your home. Each crystal has a different meaning and use. For example, some crystals can soak up negative energy and should be placed near entry and exit points in the home. Others can be helpful for amplifying energy, attracting energy or dispelling energy. Make sure you cleanse them regularly (see below).

A SIMPLE CLEANSING METHOD

I used to do this as a child, by holding crystals up to sunlight. As the sunlight hits the crystal, it's like seeing a whole world within it (especially with quartz and clearer stones).

The most effective way to cleanse a crystal is to be grounded, barefoot on grass or soil, before declaring, in your head or out loud, that the crystal is now free of lower energies and is cleansed and ready to use again. Close your eyes and visualise golden sunlight bathing the crystal and resetting the energy back to its natural state.

Crystals for healing are best when they are comfortable to hold and placed on the skin. If a crystal that you'd usually use on the body for healing and meditation is broken or damaged, you can change its purpose and nestle it in the soil of your houseplants instead.

Plants and crystals complement each other. Sit your crystal on the topsoil around the plant. Remove when watering, as some crystals such as selenite mustn't get wet. You should be fine with any of the quartz crystals, though, which won't be damaged by water.

EVERYDAY ESSENTIAL CRYSTALS

SELENITE:
Perfect for cleansing and preventing unwanted energy from entering the home. Use a selenite wand (a crystal in the shape of a wand) near your front door to help bring a fresh flow of energy into your home.

AMETHYST:
Ideal for alleviating stress, feelings of sadness, anger and dependence. Balances mood swings. Place this in your living-room area.

ROSE QUARTZ:
Perfect for creating a harmonious, loved-up vibe in your home. Place this near your bed.

CLEAR QUARTZ:
The master crystal used for divination, meditation and amplifying psychic abilities. Use it with the full moon for extra lunar power. Place anywhere in your home.

BLACK TOURMALINE:
Wards off destructive thought patterns and self-limiting beliefs and offers protection from unwanted energy. Place under your bed.

AVENTURINE:
Great to keep in your pocket for good luck, prosperity, wealth and success. Place in the kitchen or near your front door.

TIGER'S EYE:
For those days when you need a little dose of courage and inner power and to be kind to yourself. Place it near your mirror.

Witch's Doorbells

I love witch's doorbells and have many wonderful memories of going to bookshops and little hippy clothing shops as a teenager, where they were hung on the doors and would jingle as I entered. As well as being an audible indication that someone has entered the shop, their proper use is much more interesting. Bells of all shapes and sizes have been used for centuries to mark hours in the day and significant celebrations but, more importantly, they have been used as a healing tool because of the vibrations they make.

When placed by the front door, witch's doorbells reset the energy from the last person who entered the home, but they also ward off negative energy. That small yet subtle sound can send tiny little sound vibrations out into the space to create peace and harmony.

Hang your bells up near your front door, in your car, on your altar, at your desk, or near your window for further good luck and to ward off negative energy.

WHAT YOU'LL NEED:

✳ Embroidery cotton (see colour correspondences, pages 124–127)

✳ Five small brass bells (try to use odd an number)

✳ Metal ring (similar to a key ring)

✳ Smaller bells, crystal beads, feathers, charms, talismans to make it your own

PROCESS:

As you gather and braid your cottons, weave with the intention of abundance and protection. Play music or sing as you thread on the bells. This should be a happy and relaxing activity. Remember that objects hold energy, so choose your thoughts wisely whilst making your witch's doorbells.

Orgonite Spell Bottles

Orgonite is profoundly helpful to transmute negative energy, including harmful electromagnetic frequencies (EMF). It is essentially a collection of semi-precious stones, metals and other natural elements that, when combined, creates balance in the home.

Orgonite spell bottles can help to balance energy in your home. Although a pyramid-shaped bottle is often favourable, any shape will assist the orgonite to filter out unwanted EMFs.

We can use natural items easily gathered from your garden and the principles of alchemy to create an orgonite spell jar.

WHAT YOU'LL NEED:

* Small glass jars with cork lids
* Metal wire (copper, iron, steel) or aluminium foil torn into smaller strips
* Small bag of rolled or chipped crystals/gemstones
* Dried herbs or petals (lavender, rosemary, bay, chamomile, rose)
* Gold leaf (optional)

PROCESS:

Always clean out your spell bottles before you use them. Use warm water and soap if needed, allow them to dry and cleanse them by wafting smoke from a sage wand or similar cleansing herb.

Try to make a batch of these jars, because you can place them around your home in multiple spaces.

1

First, create a metal coil with your wire. Wrap it around a pencil (if the metal is flexible enough) or bend with crafting pliers, so that coil easily fits into your jar. Trim off any excess wire.

'With this metal, I place here, harmful energy will disappear.'

2

Add in your crystals/gemstones.

'With these crystals I place here, harmful energy will disappear.'

3

Add gold leaf flecks for abundance, success and courage.

'With this gold I place here, harmful energy will disappear.'

4

Finally, add in your herbs/petals. Ideally these would come from your garden or local area because they will be better programmed to suit your environment.

PLACE THE JARS IN KEY AREAS AROUND YOUR HOME, NAMELY THOSE THAT YOU SPEND A LOT OF TIME IN, LIKE YOUR BEDROOM OR LIVING ROOM. THE ORGONITE SPELL BOTTLES WILL BE PARTICULARLY EFFECTIVE WHEN PLACED NEAR ELECTRONICS OR ANYWHERE YOU FEEL THAT YOU'RE RECEIVING A LOT OF EMFS.

COLOURING ACTIVITY

'IN THIS HOME, I
WILL AWAKEN THE
MYSTIC WITHIN'

- Jo Cauldrick

RUNE ACTIVITY

Runes are divination tools that enhance psychic abilities and have been used for thousands of years. Germanic speakers, Anglo-Saxons, Scandinavians and Europeans used the rune alphabet, until Latin was adopted. The runes are generally made up of straight lines that essentially create a letterform.

Rune means 'mystery, secret or hidden meaning' and, like the Tarot, offers insights to one's journey and spiritual path. There are 24 runes, plus the blank rune known as 'Odin'.

I love runes; the alphabet is simple to draw and you can easily find small pebbles to make your own set. Traditionally runes are made using stones, but you can make them from wood too (see page 80 for cedar pendants).

If you are planning a trip to the coast, this is the perfect opportunity to collect a set of pebbles to create your own runes. You can mark them with gold craft glue or a paint such as acrylic. Add them to a drawstring bag. Don't forget to add a blank rune.

HOW TO USE YOUR RUNES

To cast your runes, it's advisable to do a
cleansing ritual (see page 18) with your
runes first. This means they are clear of any
stagnant energy from previous use.

For a daily rune cast:

1   Become present, breathe in and out three times.

2   Ask the runes to reveal guidance for today.

3   Choose a rune from your drawstring bag.

For a Three Rune cast:

1   Draw the 1st rune and place it on your left. This shows you the
    possibility in the future.

2   Draw the 2nd rune and place it on the right of the previous
    rune. This will reveal a suggested path forward.

3   Draw the 3rd rune and place it to the right of the previous rune.
    This will reveal the overall message or outcome.

RUNE MEANINGS

ᚠ **FEHU -**
Prosperity and good fortune, especially for property and finances. Your hard work is paying off. Reversed rune, means stagnation or temporary loss of good fortune.

ᚢ **URUZ -**
Strength is represented in this rune, often pertaining to a loss that will ultimately lead to a fresh start and new beginning. Reversed: Health issues, loss in strength.

ᚦ **THURISAZ -**
Protection and defences are needed at this time. Call upon friends and family to assist you. Reversed: Challenging news, feeling unsupported.

ᚨ **ANSUZ -**
Communication and insights are on their way. Expect greater awareness and knowledge to be imparted to you. Reverse: Apply discernment, not everything is as it seems.

ᚱ **RAIDHO -**
Travel and time for transformation. Personal growth and relationships can be strengthened now. Reverse: Delays in plans, or travels.

ᚲ **KENAZ -**
Clarity follows confusion and with it a sense of creativity and light. This rune also represents inner strength. Reversed: Confusion and blockages.

ᚷ **GEBO -**
Generosity and good fortune abound, especially with relationships, connections and partnerships. Reversed: Endings and separation.

ᚹ **WUNJO -**
Happiness, pleasure and contentment abound. You feel a sense of balance and connection to nature. Reversed: Unbalanced and unhappy.

N **HAGALAZ** -
Disruption and forces outside of your control. This represents a challenging period. Reversed: Delays and challenges.

↑ **NAUTHIZ** -
Need for endurance and patience is essential at this time to overcome challenges. Reversed: Move forward with caution.

| **ISA** -
Blockage is represented in this rune. In relationships, communication is blocked or comes to a standstill. Reversed: Conflict and confrontation.

◇ **JERA** -
Harvest and the fruits of your labour will come into fruition. This rune also represents the future and the idea of renewal. Reversed: Endings or blocked energy.

√ **EIHWAZ** -
New beginnings via endings are represented by this rune. Apply patience and inner strength. Reversed: Inability to move forward.

K **PERTHRO** -
Mystery and occult knowledge are linked to this rune, so use discernment. Reversed: Secrets revealed.

Y **ALGIZ** -
Defender, represented by the elk, means you will receive protection to ward off any negative energies. Reversed: Vulnerability.

S **SOWILO** -
Victory and success is yours, especially with personal goals and health. Reversed: Take care of yourself.

↑ **TIWAZ** -
Justice and honour are represented by this strong rune. You will be rewarded by your inner courage and bravery. Reversed: Potential conflict and arguments.

B **BERKANO** -
Renewal and new beginnings are afoot. The soil is fertile, growth is occurring and good news is on its way. Reversed: Stagnation and blocks.

EHWAZ -
Change is represented by the horse. Go with the flow of change and the path will feel harmonious. Reversed: Not facing up to problems.

MANNAZ -
Humanity and social order is represented by this masculine rune. A male influence may cross your path. Use community and connections to make progress. Reversed: Need for time alone.

LAGUZ -
Water and intuition go hand in hand. Trust your intuition with this feminine rune. Reversed: Emotional challenges.

DAGAZ -
Awakening and breakthrough give you the green light to move forward and progress. Reversed: Be mindful and don't rush.

INGWAZ -
Beginnings, good news and internal growth come with this rune. It's the ideal time to start something new, with this fertile masculine energy. Reversed: Stunted growth.

OTHALA -
The **Homeland** rune. This represents the essential connection to your roots, family traditions and values. Reversed: Family disputes may occur.

ODIN (BLANK RUNE) -
Fate plays a part in the ending and death of cycles in your life.

'SKY ABOVE, EARTH
BELOW, PEACE WITHIN'

- Unknown

Gentle Witch
Cleansing Wands

I was lucky enough to have a beautiful old apple tree in my garden when I was a child. In the spring when the blossom arrived, I used to climb to the top of the tree with my sister. We would snap off branches and make swords and wands. It was instinctive and part of our play, but now every season I create my own cleansing wands using foliage that's available around my home.

It's not necessary to have a branch for this practice; what you'll be focusing on is creating a fragrant and interesting seasonal bundle of dried foliage.

Creating a cleansing wand is a beautiful seasonal activity that you can do by gathering ingredients on your own or in a group. Think of it like magical flower arranging. As you work with the leaves and blooms, your creativity deepens, as does your magical connection to nature. Cleansing wands can be used to decorate your home, they can be laid on your altar or used to enhance spell work, where you direct the wand towards an object that you wish to place your intentions into.

The herbs and branches that I've recommended here are only suggestions; it's much better to use plants that are in season and local to your climate and location.

Please note that these wands are not for burning.

WHAT YOU'LL NEED:

* Seasonal herbs and small branches of leaves (sage, bay, lavender, rosemary, eucalyptus, evergreens etc); use herbs that dry well and hold their shape as I've suggested

* Dried flowers: you can hang them to dry in an airing cupboard or purchase ready-made ones

* Garden twine or craft string

* Ribbon for decoration

MAGICAL TIP:

I ALSO LIKE TO TIE A QUARTZ CRYSTAL POINT TO THE WAND WITH THICK WIRE; IT CAN HELP DIRECT HARMONIOUS ENERGY THROUGH THE HERBS. YOU CAN ALSO ADD BEADS, CHARMS OR A TALISMAN TO THE BUNDLE.

PROCESS:

Separate your herbs into piles and take a little portion from each one until you have the desired size of wand. Hold the base of the wand and wrap it multiple times with the twine/string in a criss-cross. I like to wrap my cleansing wands by spiralling upwards until I'm nearly at the top, wrap horizontally a few times and then reverse the process to the base again and wrap tightly. Tuck the string neatly away and tie the ends before trimming them. Now you can add a decorative ribbon.

Spring Wand

RIBBON COLOURS:
Pastel, blue, lavender, yellow and green

CRYSTALS:
Amethyst, rose quartz, moonstone, aquamarine

HERBS/FLOWERS:
Daffodil, lavender, rosemary and wild greens

Summer Wand

RIBBON COLOURS:
Gold, rose pinks, greens, sunflower yellow

CRYSTALS:
Citrine, tiger's eye, amber, topaz

HERBS/FLOWERS:
Thyme, rose, peony, basil

Autumn Wand

RIBBON COLOURS:

Black, purple, silver and orange

CRYSTALS:

Onyx, carnelian, obsidian

HERBS/FLOWERS:

Chrysanthemum, rosemary, sage, calendula

Winter Wand

RIBBON COLOURS:

Ice blue, rich berry reds, deep purple

CRYSTALS:

Clear quartz, celestite, ruby, bloodstone

HERBS/FLOWERS:

Thistle, rosemary, mistletoe, holly, sage

The Witch's House Poem

Dear home I appreciate you so
for you are my refuge, the place I know
Familiar are you, where comfort is found
Where my magic is conjured, where love abounds

Friends and family, nature spirits too
Are all welcome here as the moon is new
Dearest home, I appreciate you so
For you protect me from the wind and snow

When I leave you, blessings I do give
And return grateful for this place in which I live
I will care for you, as you do for me
And no negative energy there will be.

On each full moon, I'll adorn this place
With flowers and incense to delight the space
And with each season, an energy new
Dear home, magic will imbue.

Miniature Besoms

Besoms are brooms. When I was younger, I secretly wished I could fly on one through the woods at the back of my childhood home. Traditionally they are made from birch branches and an ash/oak staff, but you can make smaller versions too. I often make these miniature ones (especially during Samhain) to represent the banishing of stagnant energy and to sweep away old thought patterns that hold me back.

Besoms are synonymous with folklore, witches and fae. During Beltane, a pagan fertility festival on 1 May, a traditional ritual that's performed is 'broom jumping' — it is often used to symbolise the banishing of negative energy or to celebrate a sacred union between two people.

Samhain is also a key time to use, make and create besoms to honour and protect the home. Samhain is a pagan festival that takes place on the 31st October. It honours the dead and is considered to be the witches' New Year. On the 'Wheel Of The Year' it lies opposite Beltane and is the third of the harvest festivals.

What I love about making your own besom is the creative possibilities they unlock in your magical practices.

Door broom

Make a little broom that sits on your porch or by your front door. Witches often use the broom as a symbolic tool when it's not physically being used. In this case, a small broom will be ornamental.

Kitchen

You can make a few of your favourite herb-inspired besoms and hang them up with your pans.

Bedroom

You could make a little lavender and obsidian besom and lie it under your bed to enhance a good night's sleep and dispel bad dreams.

WHEEL OF THE YEAR

NORTHERN HEMISPHERE

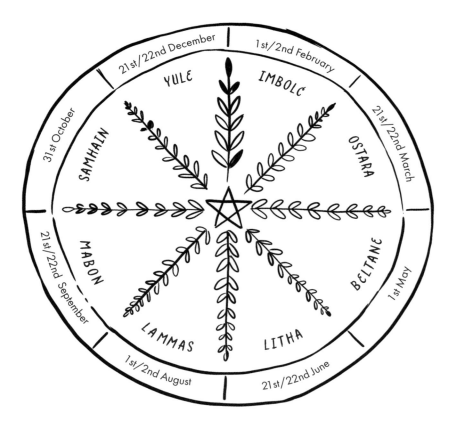

21st/22nd December

1st/2nd February

31st October

21st/22nd March

YULE

IMBOLC

SAMHAIN

OSTARA

MABON

BELTANE

21st/22nd September

1st May

LAMMAS

LITHA

1st/2nd August

21st/22nd June

COLOUR IN YOUR WHEEL OF THE YEAR,
AS EACH SEASON COMES AND GOES.

SOUTHERN HEMISPHERE

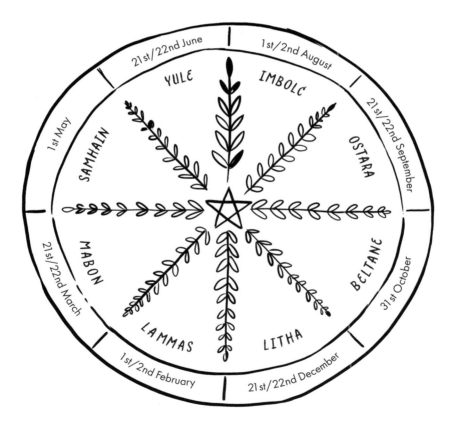

WHAT YOU'LL NEED:

* Foraged or fallen wood for the broom handle/staff is the absolute best. When you set the intention of making a besom, the wood will show up for you. If you don't have access to oak or ash, find something similar, such as a pine rod or bamboo cane. Choose a length of about 25–30 cm (10 x 12 in).

* Bunch of birch twigs or twig-like herbs (thyme, rosemary, mugwort) for the brush part of the besom. They should be 25–30 cm (10 x 12 in) long so you can trim them down to size later.

* Strong pair of scissors

* Waxed cord/string and craft wire for securing the broom

* Sigils (see page 50), talismans or anything that holds magic and meaning for you.

* Dried flowers or herbs

* Your favourite crystal

USE THIS PROCESS FOR MAKING YOUR BESOM/BROOM. YOU CAN SAND AND THEN WAX YOUR STAFF (BROOM HANDLE) BEFORE THESE STEPS.

PROCESS:

1

Take your bunch of birch twigs (and/or herbs) with the ends facing down. Grasp them tightly and cut them so they are all the same length.

2

Lay the twigs down carefully, so the cut ends come roughly a third of the way up the staff. You may need to cut a few times to get the correct length brush.

3

When you've got the desired size, wrap cord/string/wire multiple times around the brush material so it's secure.

4

Add a smaller bundle of dried flowers over the top of the brush and secure.

5

Attach a crystal or favourite talisman for even more magic at the front of the floral bundle.

To make autumnal kitchen decorative brooms, you can take sprigs of rosemary or pine needles and tie to the bottom of a cinnamon stick. I love doing this and it brings the kitchen to life.

CONNECTION

CHAPTER 2

Connection is essential when creating a wonderfully witchy home. Often you will find that you intuitively place objects around your home based on how you feel about them. Objects that hold a special memory for you will offer you a deeper connection, as will the act of crafting or making something yourself.

Using natural materials and objects, such as crystals, wood, stones and natural fibres, will also bring a magical connection into your home.

Paying attention to the seasons and the lunar cycle will help you build rhythm and deepen your magical confidence.

Rescue-Remedy Crystal Grids

A crystal grid is when you place certain crystals and natural objects together in a pattern on a flat surface. Sacred geometric patterns are followed when creating a crystal grid, because they reflect the natural mathematical ratios of all living things.

When you use crystals and sacred geometry together, you can create some beautiful grids that harmonise the ambience in your home and actually amplify the good vibes that you are seeking in your life. Collecting locally foraged plants, sticks, stones and quartz is just as lovely and they also hold the magic and memory of the environment they were discovered in. Adding leaves, berries, feathers, shells and flower petals to your grids will also have the desired effect.

I had a huge collection of stones, crystals and gemstones growing up, and my daughters also would instinctively collect chunks of quartz on our daily walks. There's something about crystals that sparks our imagination and our love of collecting. It was only when I was a teenager that I learnt about their magical potential from a woman who owned a crystal shop.

A rule of thumb is: the crystal chooses you. Invest wisely in good-quality crystals and take good care of them. It's easy to want to have a museum-worthy collection, but often all you need is a select few that you can easily use on a daily basis.

I RECOMMEND:

1 **FOR ENHANCING ENERGY**, use a large quartz crystal with a flat base for use in a space where you are interested in enhancing/amplifying something. So, for example, you could create a crystal grid on a mantelpiece or small table, with the focus being on abundance, good luck, or to bless the room.

2 **FOR SUPPORTING ENERGY**, I recommend gathering a collection of smooth rolled citrine, rose quartz, quartz, tourmaline or tiger's eye for your bath rituals.

3 **FOR PROTECTION ENERGY**, gather stones that banish bad dreams and help neutralise negativity, such as obsidian, labradorite, amazonite or moonstone. Mini crystal grids that fit neatly into small spaces can be created for this.

4 **FOR GUIDANCE AND DIRECTION**, I like amethyst, aventurine, hematite and carnelian.

Here are three simple grids that you can
replicate and use for different purposes.

1. SPIRAL

This is one of the oldest and most sacred
of symbols. It holds the resonance of
regeneration and it represents the cyclical
nature of life and death. Use this grid to
amplify your happiness and health, for your
more vibrant self.

2. SEED OF LIFE

Seed of life: this grid has seven circles that
interlink to reveal a six-petal flow in the
middle. This powerful sacred shape can
be used to increase your ability to manifest
and build motivation and inner strength.

3. VESICA PISCIS

This is one of my most favourite grid shapes to use. It represents the womb of the Universe and the link between the spiritual and physical worlds. You can make the grid outside in your back garden, on the beach, in the woods, or on your altar at home. It's very practical and versatile. Use it to bring back balance, harmony and deeper connection to your true essence and higher self.

There are few elements of best practice to think about when using your crystal grids:

★ Always use your intuition when selecting crystals and natural elements for your grid; your imagination is powerful.

★ Practise spiritual hygiene as much as you can. Clear the space you're working on, wash your hands, be present and don't rush. This is a slow and sacred activity.

★ You can easily cleanse your stones with smoke from dried herbs that are local to you or with an organic incense stick.

★ Set your intentions by deciding the purpose of the grid and how you want it to work for you.

Everyday Sigils

Sigils are markings that hold magic and meaning. We are surrounded daily by symbols that we don't often realise hold a resonance and a purpose, such as popular brand logos and icons. Simply put, sigils are markings that hold a meaning for whoever creates them, based on their intended use. They can then be used to assist you in manifesting.

I use sigils instinctively, and I have vivid memories of making up my own secret sigils in my schoolbooks. Practically, sigils can help your subconscious mind associate a symbol with an action, which is very helpful when you need to slow down, take a break, focus or trigger your subconscious mind to remember something important.

For your home, sigils can be wonderful for enhancing your magical practice.

DIFFERENT TYPES OF SIGILS AND IDEAS OF HOW YOU CAN USE THEM IN YOUR HOME:

1   The most obvious and fun sigils are those that represent zodiac signs, stars, moon phases, the sacred elements and geometry, to name a few. These can be called '**corresponding sigils**' that assist your memory.

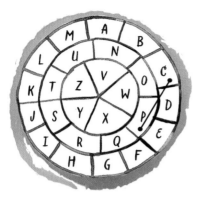

2   Another popular way to create sigils is by using the 'witches' wheel', where you place the alphabet within three rings (as shown here). You choose a word, for example PEACE and remove the vowels or repeated letters to reveal a simplified version – in this example, 'PC'. Then you plot this on your witches' wheel and the shape that remains after connecting the letters is your sigil.

3   My favourite way to create sigils, however, is to draw simple shapes that come to me during meditation, relaxation or when I walk in nature. You can create pretty flower/herb sigils that remind you of certain plant remedies or medicines; for example, you might draw a simple sigil of a yarrow plant corresponding to a healthy heart and circulatory system. Making your own version of these will help you tap into the plant medicine energy. I call these 'meditation sigils'.

Make sigils of your own by playing with combinations of hand-drawn/painted lines. A sigil is a marking you've made that holds meaning and a memory, so doodling in your notebook is a great way of playing around with ideas.

WATER CHARMING

Water charming is a way of slowing the pace down, being present and enjoying working with the sacred element of water. When you treat water with respect and show gratitude for it, you essentially programme it with a happy vibration. This is so good for you and your home environment.

Remember that you are made up of approximately 60 per cent water; if water is affected by the way it is treated, then your actual thoughts can enhance or harm you.

WATER CHARMING METHOD

Begin to pay attention to the vessels you use for water in your home. What do you drink from? Is it optimised for your health? Could you make any changes? For example, maybe you want to use glass instead of plastic.

For plants:

Choose a vessel just for watering your plants. On my watering can, I've written 'healthy, strong, abundant', which programmes the water each and every time I tend to my garden.

For your home:

If you can, use a natural filter that comes directly through to your taps; if not, use a good filter system to remove harmful added chemicals from your water. Remember to be grateful for the flow of water. You can cleanse water with a crystal wand, too. Do this by setting a clear intention to put the life force back into the water and make it optimised for health.

For drinks:

A method I was taught by a spiritualist is to always mix your drink clockwise for abundance and health – think of the 'spiral' in sacred symbology.

21 THINGS *l* LOVE ABOUT
★ MY LIFE ★

1 _____

2 _____

3 _____

4 _____

5 _____

6 _____

7 _____

8 _____

9 _____

10 _____

11 _____

12 _____

13 _____

14 _____

15 _____

16 _____

17 _____

18 _____

19 _____

20 _____

21 _____

COLOURING ACTIVITY

Enjoy colouring in these magical bottles
of Air, Fire, Earth and Water.

Air

Fire

Earth

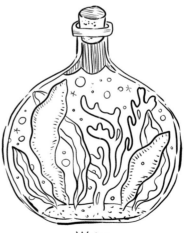

Water

MUSIC AND SOUND IN YOUR HOME

The music you play, and the sounds of your home and environment play a big part in the resonance that affects your body and the natural elements around you. Pay attention to this, especially if you feel out of balance.

Certain materials and objects can make natural sounds and your body will be affected by this.

Wind chimes:

Bamboo chimes have a deeper, hollower tone – as opposed to metal wind chimes, which can be quite uncomfortable to the ear. If you're looking for chimes for your home and garden, make sure it's a sound you feel comfortable with and could listen to often.

Also see the 'Witch's Doorbells' practice on page 22.

Singing bowls:

Singing bowls are also known as Tibetan singing bowls and they produce a sound vibration when a mallet or striker touches the bowl. There is a huge variation in types of bowls, from vintage metal varieties to more new-age crystal designs. Each bowl has a different tone, and those tones are used for different purposes. For example, high tones would be more suited for physical healing, whereas lower tones will help with grounding and stress relief.

Running water:

There's no reason why you can't incorporate a little solar-powered mini fountain in your home, by putting it in a bucket or bowl of water and adding some water-loving plants. The sound of water is so healing and comforting. If you don't have a garden, you can create a mini paradise inside your home.

432 Hz music:

Music always evokes emotions and one of the most effective ways to relax, especially when you are feeling stressed, is to listen to music that is tuned to 432 Hz. Both hemispheres of the brain synchronise when listening to 432 Hz and this encourages creativity and intuition.

Witch's Journey Sticks

Life is a journey and what better way to mark significant milestones in your life than with a journey stick? The principle of the witch's journey stick is to symbolically mark times in your life where something memorable has happened to you – in particular, something you've grown from or a challenge you've overcome. It is also an invitation to create memories. Traditionally you might choose to have a photo album that lives in a box under your sofa. By creating a witch's journey stick, you can see where you're at and what you'd like to add next.

I've used these throughout my life and with my children, as a crafting activity. What I particularly love about them is that they start with the choosing of just the right stick – which is a mini adventure in itself. When you set the intention to make a journey stick, it won't be long before the Universe and tree spirits provide the perfect stick for you.

WHAT YOU'LL NEED:

* Foraged stick that's not rotten and has some strength to it
* Fine sandpaper
* Embroidery threads in various colours
* Acrylic paint
* Paintbrush
* Ribbons

PROCESS:

1 Choose your branch/stick and sand down any rough areas.

2 Welcome your journey stick into your home and find a suitable place for it. Like a witch's broom, journey sticks are a lovely addition to your space.

3 You can have a collection of different-sized journey sticks; perhaps shorter ones to create a witch's journey stick as a complete project and longer ones to be added to over a longer period of time.

4 Think of your magical sticks like a collection of wands, which you build up over time. The colour used holds significance, too; choose colours that represent a feeling or an aesthetic you want. Wrap the cord/thread around the branch. Push the threads together to create distinctive bands. You can paint bands instead of using threads.

5 If you are reflecting on an event, for example a new job, moving home or welcoming in a new family member, you can use your witch's journey stick to record this event. Add little gift tags with a date to your thread or sew in beads to give it more texture and interest.

6 You can also mark a date on the wood, use a special sigil or punch holes into tags and photos to hang on the branch.

7 Display your witch's journey stick as you would a wall hanging, or store upright in a special corner in your home.

222

666

ANGEL NUMBERS

999

Numerology is an occult science and a method of divination that is used to understand the sacred relationship between numbers and their meanings.

Have you seen repeating numbers or numbers that show up in a particular sequence? Many people experience this and it's often attributed to an awakening of consciousness.

When you see certain numbers show up for you in your everyday life or experience a coincidental event that you notice is very well timed, it can give you insights about your spiritual path and indicate that you are being supported by your angels/spirit guides. Pay attention to these numbers and the messages they bring.

555

HERE ARE SOME REPEATED NUMBERS AND THEIR MESSAGES:

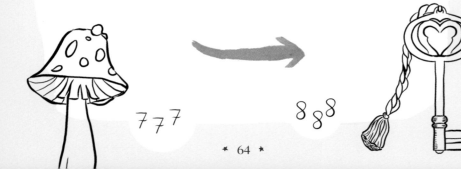

777

888

111 New Beginnings

Align with your true path, maintain optimistic and positive affirmations. Trust, nurture and expand on your inner wisdom and intuition.

222 Master Builder

Balance is the key, maintain faith and a philosophical approach to events in your life. Nothing is by accident, everything is orchestrated. Your angels are supporting you.

333 Ascended Master

The trinity of mind, body and spirit is amplified now. Growth and expansion of your imagination will assist you on your soul journey and uplift others who cross your path. The ascended masters are supporting you now.

444 Life Purpose

Maintain enthusiasm and dedication to your goals and dreams. There is nothing to fear, you are being supported and guided at this time.

555 Life Changes

You're being guided to release and let go of anything that no longer serves you and to trust that this transition will lead to long term benefits.

666 Raise the Vibration

When you see these numbers or attributes of this number, it's a call to review your attachment to material things. Focus on an abundance mindset rather than that of lack, and seek assistance from your spirit guides.

777 Awakening

You are listening and, therefore, you are spiritually evolving. The lessons you have learnt so far are helping you to be of higher service to others.

888 Spiritual Law

If you have mastered the law of karma, you will see swift blessings in the areas of finances. You are guided and supported, as this number often alludes to an ending of something. All is well.

999 Cycles Ending

For your life purpose to continue to unfold, necessary changes and endings must occur. Now is the time to embrace what you truly want to do in your life and to trust your heart.

1000 Amplifier

Numbers that include 0 will become super charged and will amplify their attributes. 0 is known as the 'God' force number, a clear space for potential growth, choices and options. This is the beginning of a spiritual journey with the energy of oneness and wholeness.

Moon-Phase Garland

This is one of my favourite witchcraft activities. I made hundreds of
these paper garlands in different colours to sell a few years ago, and
they make amazing gifts, too. The lunar cycle has eight main phases,
represented in this activity to illustrate the entire lunar cycle.

It's a beautiful home decor item that reminds you of your connection
to the moon.

Some witchy folk also like to acknowledge the dark moon, which is a
special window of time between the last light of the waning moon and
the new moon. The waning-moon phases come after the full moon and
include the balsamic moon.

The waxing moon is typically a time for attracting and momentum; this is
where the moon builds luminosity.

The waning moon is typically a time of surrendering and letting go; this is
where the moon loses its luminosity.

Once you hang these beauties up, you won't believe how lovely they
can make your space look.

 New moon

Waxing crescent

 1st quarter

Waxing gibbous

 Full moon

Disseminating moon

 3rd quarter moon

Balsamic moon

WHAT YOU'LL NEED:

* Thick craft paper that can handle acrylic paint on both sides
* Acrylic paint in metallic colours
* Mixing palette
* Paintbrush
* Old toothbrush
* A circle die cutter (the largest you can find) or cut one circle out of cardboard to use as a template
* Sewing machine, hand sewing kit or thread and a hole punch

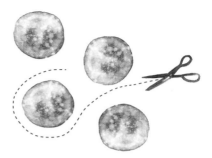

PROCESS:

When I made my garlands, I painted a whole piece of thick craft paper on both sides and let it dry before using the circular die cutter.

First, add a generous blob of acrylic paint to a paint palette. I used a variety of colours for different moon garlands. You could paint each phase a different colour, too. Then dip a folded 2 cm (¾ in) piece of cardboard into the paint and apply it in multiple directions onto the paper. I used this instead of a paintbrush because I was able to cover a large area and it gives a sense of texture. Feel free to use a paintbrush, however. When the paint dries, you can use white paint and flick the bristles of the toothbrush to create a galaxy effect on the paper.

2

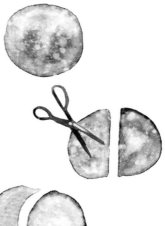

Cut four circles out of the painted paper for each garland. This creates seven moon phases (see the illustration on page 67 – the new moon isn't represented in this garland).

1 CIRCLE FOR THE FULL MOON

1 CIRCLE CUT IN HALF GIVES 2 HALF MOONS

2 CIRCLES FOR 2 CRESCENT MOONS AND LEFTOVER PAINTED PAPER CREATES A WANING GIBBOUS AND WAXING GIBBOUS MOON.

3

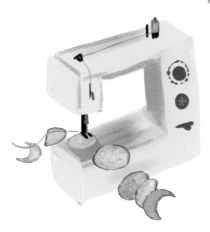

Run the middle of each circle through the sewing machine one after another to create a chain. Alternatively, you can sew through the middle by hand or use a hole punch on opposite sides of each moon phase and then thread cotton through them. This works best if you're using larger moon shapes.

If you'd like to try some other designs, you can create a wolf moon garland or have a play around with different colours and textures.

$\mathscr{H}$ARMONY

* CHAPTER 3 *

Harmony to me means multiple elements working together without the sense of restriction. I suppose it is close to the state of flow I experience when creating a painting or tending to my garden, when things seem effortless and lined up. A harmonious home is a reflection of how you feel.

Creating a harmonious home is at the core of how your living space can become a haven for magic and creativity. Nature has exquisite harmony, so by infusing your crafts, furniture, plants, candles and crystals together, you can create a truly beautiful atmosphere in your home.

We all have messy home days, that's life. The key to creating sustainable flow is having beautiful rituals that help you stay on top of your household tasks and replenish the positive energy on a regular basis. Consistency is key; when you feel disorganised, it's likely that you have spaces in your home that need attention.

The new moon is also an opportunity to clear out items from your home that no longer serve. This way you are inviting fresh new possibilities into your home and extra room for creative magic.

House Blessing

Blessing your home, or someone else's, does not have to be a formal affair. It's good to practise spiritual hygiene when entering your home. Wipe your feet and remove your shoes.

A house blessing shows that you are grateful and you are already living in a state of abundance. The home knows your energy.

WHAT YOU'LL NEED:

* Yourself! And to be in a calm, happy and clear-minded mood
* Cleansing wand (see Gentle Witch Cleansing Wands on page 34)
* Your favourite crystal
* A clear, clean space on the floor to sit down

PROCESS:

Perform this house blessing in your home. Firstly take off your shoes, then sit down on the floor, with your hands touching the ground.

Focus on feeling happy and grateful for your home. Focus on the feeling you get from being in a place that makes you feel safe and loved. When you visualise, you are watching a movie playing out in your mind of the way you see or would like to see your house.

Cleaning your space first shows your home respect. If things are misaligned in the home, this is also the perfect time to do a blessing.

Carefully burn your cleansing wand.

Work in circular clockwise motions to increase abundance. Place the wand on a heatproof dish and begin the blessing.

Whilst in a kneeling position, place both hands on the floor in front of you. Close your eyes and repeat this out loud or to yourself.

Imagine a beautiful golden light emanating from you like a ripple in a pond. The ripple reaches all four corners of your home. As you focus on thoughts of protection and stability, imagine that golden light pulsing out far beyond your home, into your neighbours' homes and the wider village, town, city and country.

Feel the feeling of the house already being abundant in all areas. See your home as safe, secure and a place where you can be yourself.

'Hello, dear home,
I love and appreciate you

May this space be blessed
With harmony and abundance

I thank you for your protection
I am grateful for this space.'

Witch's Herb Wall Hanging

No witch's home would be complete without a simple yet practical herb hanging. It will immediately uplift the room; the plants will cleanse the environment and it will create that gorgeous witchy aesthetic that keeps your home looking and feeling inspirational.

I've been making these for years and they are surprisingly simple to construct. You can hang them in any suitable space. Find a spare wall, use a picture hook to hang a branch on and, as if by magic, you have somewhere to begin hanging and drying your witchy herbs.

WHAT YOU'LL NEED:

* A lovely piece of wood that ideally you've acquired whilst out on a nature walk or in your garden. If you can't find what you're looking for, a bamboo cane is a great alternative.

* Cotton twine/garden string

* A wall screw or picture hook/nail

* Herbs: I recommend locally foraged ones that hold their shape well, such as lavender, sage, bay, curry plant, yarrow and rosemary

* String or elastic for the herbs

* Scissors

PROCESS:

1 Tie string securely to each end of your stick, making sure there's enough string to allow the stick to hang naturally down from the wall screw or picture hook.

2 Select small bunches of herbs to tie. Elastic is helpful because it will contract as the herbs lose water and dry up. String is also fine, you may just need to tighten it up later on.

3 Hang your herbs at various lengths for interest and so they don't bump against each other. Allow them to dry for a couple of weeks.

4 A lovely way to add some more magic to your wall hanging is to drape and twist foliage around the stick. I use eucalyptus, but you can use laurel, fir, holly or ivy and this can all be found for free in your garden or out on walks.

5 Drape vintage lace or ribbons to add to the aesthetic.

GUIDED MEDITATION

This is your time to connect to your higher self, to the Universe and to all that is around you. Find a quiet space, get comfortable and close your eyes.

. . . .

With each breath in imagine, light, wisdom and compassion flooding in, and with exhalation imagine releasing any worries, stresses or concerns you have.

Become aware of that stillness as you invite in light and let go of the pressures you place onto yourself. Now let's invite the loving energy of Hestia, keeper of the fire, Goddess of the Hearth and Home.

Be still now and connect to the silence within.
The hum of the Universe is comforting, like the beat of a happy heart.
As the cosmos expands, you see millions of stars wrapped up in blankets of more stars.
As your breath takes you deeper into the subconscious realms, you see a tiny glowing light in the distance.

You focus on this.

As the light gets closer, you notice it is being held
by the great Goddess of the Hearth and Home, Hestia.

She passes you the flame of love and protection.
You carefully receive this and place it into your heart.
You nurture and care for this flame within, your heart now glows with a warm, loving light.
This light pulses through the molecules of your being and regenerates your mind.

Now you feel the love flowing through you.

Breathe in.

You are powered by the eternal love of source energy, the brave glowing fire within burns off the toxicity of limited beliefs and instead becomes the fuel you need to be the keeper of your own flame.

Now repeat these affirmations as you sit by your own fire/lit candle.

★

I am a divine spark of creative energy.
I am curious and use this to enhance my imagination.
I pull inspiration from many, many places.
I am not limited by what I can invent and make.
I give myself permission now to experiment with ideas I've been dreaming up for so long.
When I show up for my creative side, I feed and nourish myself
I am a creative being.
When I pour loving energy into my home, it becomes a haven for my creativity.
My home is safe and strong.
I am so grateful for my home.

★

Full Moon Cake

It's quite the loveliest thing to make your cake on the day of a full moon. To make it even more aligned with the seasons, choose a cake recipe that includes fruit that's available in your geographical region, or better still, use fruit that you've grown. Make your cake on the day of the full moon to attract the most magic.

★ Clear all surfaces and prepare baking equipment.

★ Put some of your favourite music on.

★ Set an intention to make a lovely cake. I am not a great baker, but I always set the intention that I am and that I will make a scrumptious cake that my family will enjoy.

★ An idea given to me by a friend of mine some years ago, is to write an affirmation or power word on edible rice paper and add it to your cake mix before you bake your Full Moon Cake.

★ Take your time and enjoy the process.

★ Decorate your Full Moon Cake with edible flowers, or dress a table like you would your altar and place the cake in the centre.

★ Before eating, it's a good idea to bless the cake. I always bless my cake with abundance, as if every slice is magically charged with love and good luck.

You could have a Full Moon Cake party with friends or take turns theming the cake. For the Equinox cakes, I like to decorate half the cake in chocolate to represent the darkness and half the cake with white/cream icing to represent the sun.

Pebble Painting

I remember vividly collecting stones as a child. I wanted them all. I particularly liked the flat, smooth ones. Later, as a teenager during the summer breaks, I would sit outside and paint stones that I'd gathered on walks, as gifts for my family.

You can take this pebble-painting activity to the next magical level.

WHAT YOU'LL NEED:

* Smooth, flat pebbles
* Acrylic paint
* Acrylic pens
* Acrylic fixing varnish
* Paintbrush

Here are some ideas for creating a vast array of stunning pebbles.

Paint or draw power words – also known as affirmation words – on the stones. Writing a 'power' word really does help to reinforce it. The act of using paint on a natural surface such as a stone is calming and absorbing.

Create stones that represent goddesses to display on your altar.

Paint spirit animals from your dreams.

Make seasonal pebble collections, such as naming all the *pagan sabbats.

*PAGAN SABBATS FOLLOW THE SUN AND THE SEASONS TO MARK KEY DATES BETWEEN THE LONGEST AND SHORTEST DAYS OF LIGHT (MIDSUMMER AND YULE). FESTIVALS ARE FOCUSED ON HARNESSING THE POWER OF SPRING, SUMMER, AUTUMN AND WINTER, EMPOWERING US TO HAVE A DEEPER AWARENESS OF OUR CONNECTION TO NATURE AND EACH OTHER.

Create magical sigil designs in gold and silver paint.

The Ringing Cedar Pendant

In 2012 I embarked on a journey with my family to the south of France. It was our intention to join an eco-community and build an earth home. This didn't come into fruition; however, I was given a book called *The Ringing Cedars of Russia*. Cedar pendants are designed to be worn around your neck and you're encouraged to rub the pendant to transfer the natural oils from your finger onto the wood. This imprints the pendant with your unique fingerprint, oils and energy.

Wearing a natural item such as this makes you feel relaxed and less anxious. Over time the pendant will naturally darken with your oils and become more fragrant.

I made my first pendant from a branch of a cedar pine that was on the land I was living on. I still have it today. The more you wear it and touch the pendant, the darker the wood turns.

Don't worry if you don't have cedar; finding fallen branches from your local region is just as good.

Here is a list of woods that will make good pendants.

Olive

Apple

Cherry

Ash

Hawthorn

Oak

WHAT YOU'LL NEED:

* Fallen, seasoned (left to dry/season) branch about 2 cm (¾ in) in diameter
* Clamp
* A small hand saw
* Coarse-grade sandpaper for sanding
* Fine-grade sandpaper for finishing and polishing
* Any non-toxic and natural wood oil, such as olive oil or linseed
* A drop of cedar essential oil or preferred scent
* Old cotton cloth or flannel
* Small hand drill
* Silver chain, leather cord or natural string

PROCESS:

1

Choose a branch that is fairly straight, to maximise how many coins you can get from the branch.

2

Clamp and saw your wood into coins that are about 5 mm (¼ in) thick.

3

Sand down the back and front of the coins using coarse-grade sandpaper. Enjoy the process of sanding down. Use fine/medium-grade sandpaper and rub in circular motions to smooth and polish the wood.

4

Finish by oiling the pendant. With an old cotton cloth or flannel, dip it into linseed/olive oil/other natural wood oil and gently run into the pendant. Allow to fully dry between applications. I recommend adding several coats. Add drops of scented oil during this process.

5

There are several ways you can create your pendant. You can drill a hole vertically through the wooden coin, or horizontally from front to back. You can also screw in a jewellery eyelet to attach a chain to.

COLOURING ACTIVITY

WRITE A POWER WORD IN THE BASKET

'I AM A CHILD OF THE MOON, RAISED BY THE SUN IN A WORLD WALKED BY STARS AND A SKY DRAWN WITH FLOWERS'

- Zara Ventris

The Fortune Teller

When I was talking about this book to my bestie, she immediately suggested an 'inner child' activity called the 'fortune teller' (aka 'cootie catcher'). I fondly remember making these paper shapes a lot as a child. I would use them to ask my friends questions and we'd discover the answers together. There's a simple and nostalgic magic to paper crafts.

A 'fortune teller' is essentially a square piece of paper folded into a 3D shape that you can move with your fingers. The main idea is to ask a recipient to select different options they see on the fortune teller, which then reveals a fun challenge or a fortune.

There are so many variations you could make, such as:

What's your Animal Ally?

What is your Destiny Number, which is thought to be linked to your life path?

A message from the Universe.

WHAT YOU'LL NEED:

* A square piece of paper.
* Pen and colouring pens

PROCESS:

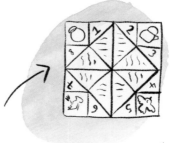

1

Referring to the illustration on page 89, add four separate images to the corners on one side of your square. Then add the eight numbers in the triangles. Finally write a message in each of the eight centre triangles – these can be a thought for the day or message of support.

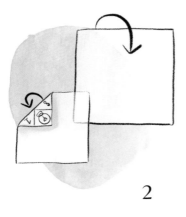

2

Turn over the square and fold all four corners inwards to meet in the middle. All points should be touching, but not perfectly.

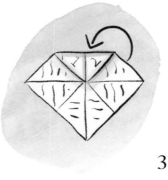

3

Turn the whole square back over and repeat step 2.

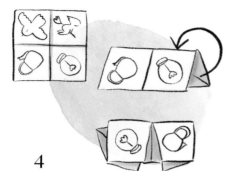

4

Flip your square over once again and fold in half each way.

5

Place your index fingers and thumbs from each hand under the left and right corner flaps.

6

You may need to fiddle a bit to get the paper to open and close in the two directions, like a little bird beak.

HOW TO READ THE FORTUNES:

1. CHOOSE A PICTURE FROM LAYER ONE AND OPEN AND SHUT THE FORTUNE TELLER AS YOU SPELL OUT THE WORD. FOR EXAMPLE, FOR AN 'OWL' YOU'D OPEN AND SHUT IT THREE TIMES.

2. PICK A NUMBER FROM THE SECOND LAYER. OPEN AND SHUT THE FORTUNE TELLER THIS NUMBER OF TIMES.

3. CHOOSE A SECOND NUMBER, BUT THIS TIME DIRECTLY OPEN THE CORRESPONDING FLAP. THIS WILL REVEAL YOUR MESSAGE.

DAY

Your morning energy can powerfully inform how the rest of your day will evolve. The morning holds possibilities of what is to come. Cultivate rituals in your daily routine to increase positive energy, and maybe do something a bit more special when you have time off or more space away from regular work or commitments.

Each day of the week holds a different energy and association, so you may want to utilise this energy to plan a special, magical day that is slower paced or that you can be more intentional about.

The daytime is where you can utilise the sun's energy, especially in and around the home. This is the time when a witch can clean the home, sweep with the broom and invite fresh new energy into the living space.

MAGICAL MORNING HABITS

Making a decision about how you want to start your day is so powerful. Today is a fresh start, a clean slate; it's an opportunity to worry not about yesterday but instead set a new intention for the day ahead. A witch's home is a sanctuary for rest and inspired action, so how do you want to craft your magical morning?

Opposite I've made some suggestions based on what I do, but you can create your own habits.

1

A morning stretch can invigorate your body
and gently wake it up.

2

Warm water and lemon can help promote healthy
digestion and will rehydrate you after sleep.

3

Writing for five minutes in a journal can help you
release anything you've been holding from the
previous day. You can set a powerful intention
about how you want your day to go, or record
three things you're grateful for and reinforce
the goals you are currently working towards.

4

A tidy place makes for a more creative space.
Cleaning your home regularly will refresh
the energy and make it a more harmonious
environment.

Days of the Week Spells

Each day of the week is ruled by a different celestial body and has many connections to herbs, trees, astrological signs, colours and symbols.

You can harness and utilise the unique energy of each day of the week to create rituals or themed spells. I like to refer to these daily spells as a dose of practical magic to use at will, when you feel a spark of inspiration or when you want to focus on something specific.

WHAT YOU'LL NEED:

* Coloured candles (birthday candles are a great alternative). These colours will link to each day of the week. Please note that when the spell requires you to wait until the candle has completely burnt down, this is not always practical; in which case, light the candle and watch it burn for three minutes to reinforce the magic.

* Salt

* Your preferred essential oil or one that corresponds with the day of the week

* Oil burner for water and essential oils. Add drops of essential oil to the water placed on top of the burner. Then light a tea light (uncoloured is fine) underneath to gently heat the water and release the aromas.

* Little squares of either cartridge paper or standard paper

* Set of ink pens in various colours

* Corresponding crystal or clear quartz

* A mirror

SUNDAY

Sunday is ruled by the Sun, and it is a great day to focus your spells on attracting abundance, happiness, health or creativity.

COLOUR:
Gold or yellow

CRYSTAL:
Amber, carnelian, topaz

INCENSE AND OILS:
Cinnamon, rosemary, frankincense

Use a yellow/gold candle on a gold-coloured plate. Encircle it with a line of salt for protection. If you have any yellow flowers, add these around the edge. Light the oil burner and add some essential oil drops. Light the candle and focus on what abundance (for example) feels like in your life. Breathe in and out 20 times.

Pause and sit for a moment. Now you may write down on a square piece of paper with yellow or gold ink what it is you're looking to attract into your life.

If you don't know what to write, use a *disc* symbol or sigil. Fold the paper over three times to reinforce the magic and place your crystal over the top of it. Wait for three minutes whilst the candle burns and then cleanse and tidy up the space.

Repeat out loud or in your mind three times: *'On this blessed day, may abundance, health and happiness come into play.'*

MONDAY

Monday is ruled by the Moon, and it is a great day to focus on areas like dream-work, which is your ability to use your vast imagination during sleep and meditation. The moon is also associated with the subconscious mind, emotions and fertility.

COLOUR:
Lilac, silver, white

CRYSTAL:
Moonstone, selenite, pearl

INCENSE AND OILS:
Jasmine, sandalwood, moonwort, star anise, myrrh gum

Place a white candle on a plate (any colour/type will do). Encircle it with a line of salt for protection. If you have any moon water (see page 130), sprinkle some around the candle and on the paper, otherwise use salt. Light the oil burner and add some essential oil drops. Light the candle in front of a mirror and focus on that which you can feel rather than what you see.

Breathe in and out 20 times. Pause and sit for a moment. Now you may write down on a square piece of paper what it is you want the energy of the moon to reveal to you.

If you don't know what to write, use a *cauldron* symbol or sigil. Fold the paper three times to reinforce the magic and place a crystal over the top of it. The best time to do this spell would be under a full or waning moon. Wait until the candle has completely burnt down and then cleanse and tidy up the space.

Repeat out loud or in your mind three times: *'On this blessed day, may my intuition and imagination lead the way.'*

TUESDAY

Tuesday is ruled by Mars, and it is a great day to focus on attracting success or achieving a particular goal or adding a spark of motivation to your day.

COLOUR:
Red/orange

CRYSTAL:
Bloodstone, garnet, carnelian

INCENSE AND OILS:
Sandalwood, cinnamon, frankincense

Place a red candle on a plate. Encircle it with a line of salt for protection. Light the oil burner and add some essential oil drops. Light the candle and focus on what you are hoping to attract.

Breathe in and out 20 times. Pause and sit for a moment. Now you may write down on a square piece of paper the area of your life in which you need a spark of motivation or success. If you don't know what to write, use an *arrow* symbol (representing action) or sigil.

Fold the paper three times to reinforce the magic and place a crystal over the top of it. The best time to do this spell would be under a full or waxing moon.

Wait until the candle has completely burnt down and then cleanse and tidy up the space. Repeat out loud or in your mind three times:
'On this blessed day, may success and motivation come into play.'

WEDNESDAY

Wednesday is ruled by Mercury, so a good focus for your spells would be anything associated with divination, communication, knowledge and business.

> *COLOUR:*
> Yellow
>
> *CRYSTAL:*
> Yellow jasper, quartz, opal
>
> *INCENSE AND OILS:*
> Star anise, lavender, liquorice

Place a yellow candle on a plate. Encircle it with a line of salt for protection. Light the oil burner and add some essential oil drops.

Light the candle and breathe in and out 20 times. Pause and sit for a moment. Now you may write down on a square piece of paper what it is you want to solve, remedy or attract.

If you don't know what to write, use a *staff* symbol (representing focus) or sigil. Fold the paper three times to reinforce the magic and place a crystal over the top of it. Leave for at least 24 hours. The best time to do this spell would be just before you have an interview or important event that requires your concentration and focus.

Wait until the candle has completely burnt down and then cleanse and tidy up the space. Repeat out loud or in your mind three times: *'On this blessed day, may clarity and connection come into play.'*

THURSDAY

Thursday is ruled by Jupiter, so this is the ideal time to try spells that are focused on success, career, family, spiritual growth and expansion.

> **COLOUR:**
> Purple/dark blue
>
> **CRYSTAL:**
> Lapis lazuli, blue topaz, sapphire
>
> **INCENSE AND OILS:**
> Cedar, pine, sweet almond

Place a blue candle on a plate. Encircle it with a line of salt for protection. Light the oil burner and add some drops of essential oil.

Light the candle and breathe in and out 20 times. Pause and sit for a moment. Now you may write down on a square piece of paper what it is you want to grow, amplify or expand.

If you don't know what to write, use a *drum* symbol (representing your unique rhythm) or sigil. Fold the paper three times to reinforce the magic and place a crystal over the top of it. Wait until the candle has completely burnt down and then cleanse and tidy up the space. The best time to do this spell would be during a waxing moon.

Repeat out loud or in your mind three times: *'On this blessed day, growth and expansion come into play.'*

$\mathscr{F}$RIDAY

Friday is ruled by Venus, so this is the ideal time to try spells that are focused on love, balance, art, beauty, relationships and pleasurable delights.

COLOUR:
Green or pink

CRYSTAL:
Green fluorite, emerald, malachite

INCENSE AND OILS:
Incense and oils: lilac, raspberry, vanilla, violet

Use a green or pink candle on a plate. Encircle it with a line of salt for protection. Light the oil burner and add some drops of essential oil. Light the candle and breathe in and out 20 times. Pause and sit for a moment. Now you may write down on a square piece of paper what it is you want to attract; will it be romantic love, artistic flair, harmonious relationships or deep friendships?

If you don't know what to write, use a *rose* symbol (representing love) or sigil. Fold the paper three times to reinforce the magic and place a crystal over the top of it. Wait until the candle has completely burnt down and then cleanse and tidy up the space.

The best time to do this spell would be during a waxing moon and full moon.

Repeat out loud or in your mind three times: *'On this blessed day, may love and balance come into play.'*

SATURDAY

Saturday is ruled by Saturn, and this is the ideal time to try spells that are focused on protection, perseverance, stability, karma and detoxification.

COLOUR:
Indigo

CRYSTAL:
Smoky quartz, hematite, onyx

INCENSE AND OILS:
Cypress, dill, patchouli, rosemary

Place a blue/indigo candle on a plate. Encircle it with a line of salt for protection. Light the oil burner and add some drops of essential oil. Light the candle and breathe in and out 20 times. Pause and sit for a moment. Now you may write down on a square piece of paper what it is you want to break free from, create protection from or expel from your life.

If you don't know what to write, use a cord or chain symbol (representing protection) or sigil. Fold the paper three times to reinforce the magic and place a crystal over the top of it.

Wait until the candle has completely burnt down and then cleanse and tidy up the space. The best time to do this spell would be during a waning moon.

Repeat out loud or in your mind three times:
'On this blessed day, may any negative energies leave and not stay.'

Money-Attracting Amulet

When was the last time that you cleared out your wallet or purse? If you want to shift the energy around your ability to attract more money into your life, the first thing to do is to improve your relationship with money and the energy of wealth and abundance. This means you should respect your wallet or purse as a portal for receiving wealth.

I have been carrying a silver coin in my wallet for years; it tells my subconscious mind that I always have money and that I am provided for. You can make a personalised magical amulet that is programmed with your unique blueprint for attracting money.

This is best created when you are feeling very present and positive about your relationship with money. When you make an amulet, you will be reminded of how easily money can come to you (money flow) and that when you are without resistance, you can trust the Universe to provide for you.

If you have a strong intention of attracting a certain amount of money, then use that number in your amulet.

WHAT YOU'LL NEED:

* ✱ Gold pen and a small piece of paper
* ✱ A tiny rolled gemstone of citrine
* ✱ A dried bay leaf and three sunflower seeds
* ✱ A small square of fabric, ideally natural-fibre fabric (10 x 10 cm/4 x 4 in)
* ✱ Gold ribbon or thread (this represents the sun and prosperity)

PROCESS:

1　Lay out all the elements on a table near natural sunlight.

2　Using your gold pen, write down on the piece of paper what you have already manifested in the present moment. For example, 'I am so grateful for the money that continues to support me and flow in my direction.' Or you could write down a figure that you are focused on attracting.

3　Fold the paper three times (to reinforce the magic).

4　Add a crystal on top, followed by the bay leaf and sunflower seeds.

5　Gather the square of fabric into a bag shape, including all the items in the bag, and tie it three times with the gold ribbon or thread.

6　Close your eyes and breathe in and out 20 times, whilst placing your hands on the bag.

7　Cleanse the amulet by using a cleansing wand (see page 34) before placing it into your wallet or purse.

A YEAR OF MAGICAL ALTARS

Wicca uses spiritual traditions to express the sacred relationship of a self-led religion, without formal rules. It has a strong focus on nature and cultivating one's own magical confidence, which means it's accessible to many aspiring witches or those who are just looking for a deeper connection to themselves and the natural world around them. Wicca embraces the cyclical nature of inner and outer growth, that which lies within us and how our practices and beliefs can shape the outside world.

The eight sabbats (holidays or festivals) of the year are based on ancestral traditions that harness energy at key points during the solar year, and they are depicted as a wheel. Creating an altar in your home is a beautiful way to celebrate each of the sabbats. It brings a new aesthetic to your living space, which sparks further creativity and your magical relationship to spirit and nature.

Here is an invitation to colour in and decorate these eight sabbat-inspired altars. This is a mindfulness activity, but also one that will help you remember the names and timings of the sabbats, should you wish to celebrate them and create your own themed altars. I've included the approximate dates associated with these nature festivals; however, the celebratory energy is designed to be observed for a month at least and it will depend on where you are situated in the world.

SAMHAIN: falls between the autumn equinox and yule.

Samhain is the 'Festival of the Dead', and for witches it's a truly magical time where ancestors can be honoured and the Crone Goddess who represents the cycles of life and death can be celebrated. Samhain, in its simplicity, heralds 'change' and that winter is just around the corner. Samhain is celebrated on 31st October (1st May in the southern hemisphere).

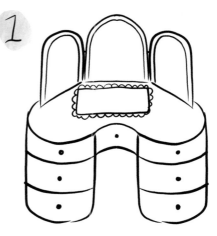

YULE/WINTER SOLSTICE: 21st/22nd Dec (21st/22nd June in the southern hemisphere)

Yule is also referred to as midwinter and marks the shortest day of light in the year. This means that the darkest days will soon be over and sun will return. Hearty and warm celebrations with friends and family are enjoyed at this time. The witch pays attention to the evergreen plants and trees and creates new projects and ideas during a more fallow time.

IMBOLC: 1st/2nd February (1st/2nd August in the southern hemisphere)

Imbolc (pronounced im-ol-c) marks the returning of light and life. Little shoots begin to appear and the first lambs of the year are born. St Brigid the Goddess of Metalwork, Midwifery, Poetry and Creativity is honoured during this time. For witches, she symbolises the eternal flame of creativity and healing power.

OSTARA/SPRING EQUINOX: 21st/22nd March (21st/22nd September in the southern hemisphere)

The spring equinox arrives, representing the balance of light and dark. Now the focus is growth. Nature has a huge burst of energy at this time. The iconic March hares dance and box to find a mate and the ripening full moon are symbols of fertility and new ideas coming to fruition. Egg painting and a celebratory Ostara-inspired altar can be created to fully embrace this magical time of potential.

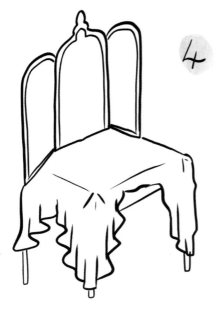

BELTANE: 1st May (31st October in the southern hemisphere)

Beltane is one of the prettiest and most colourful sabbats. It represents the coming of summer. Fires are lit to bring good will to all. May blossoms are often gathered at dusk by witches and maypoles are decorated. This is the festival associated with the union of male and female and the transition from spring to summer.

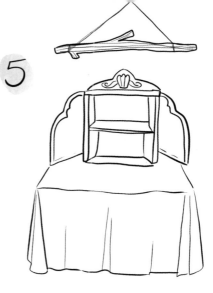

LITHA/MIDSUMMER SOLSTICE: 21st/22nd June (21st/22nd December in the southern hemisphere)

Midsummer is opposite to yule and marks the longest day of sunlight. This sabbat calls upon the sun to bring spiritual strength and deeper meaning to our life paths. Communing in places of spiritual significance – such as Stonehenge in England – are enjoyed.

LUGHNASADH OR LAMMAS: 1st/2nd August (1st/2nd February in the southern hemisphere)

Lughnasadh is the festival of the harvest and falls between the summer solstice and the autumn equinox. The fruitful summer harvests are gathered and shared with families and communities. It marks the dedication of growth and the importance of sharing one's harvest with others. For witches, the sabbat also represents a seasonal shift and a slower pace. It's a time to honour the Great Mother Gaia for the gifts of food and produce across the land.

MODRON, MABON OR THE AUTUMN EQUINOX: 21st/22nd September (21st/22nd March in the southern hemisphere)

Modron is opposite the spring equinox on the wheel, where daylight and darkness are equal. This is the time for honouring the land and enjoying colourful autumnal food. Apples feature in witches' rituals because of their symbolism: they are thought to represent the threshold between our reality and the supernatural world. As the days get shorter and the light appears to fade, this is a wildly creative time, where the focus is on preparation for winter.

'I WILL SEEK POCKETS

OF MAGIC, EVERY DAY'

- Jo Cauldrick

WHAT AREAS IN MY *HOME* NEED THE MOST ATTENTION?

WHAT WOULD I LIKE TO FOCUS ON FIRST?
HOW WILL THIS MAKE ME FEEL?

WITCH'S TOOLS

Every witch over time, will come to find a selection of
tools that help enhance their practice. Some of these are
illustrated here. Which ones are you immediately drawn to?
What would you add?

Runes

Besom

Bath Salts

Beloved Tea Pot

Cauldron

Natural Candles

Mortar & Pestle

Magical Books

Witch's Basket

Quality Crystal
Collection

Journal

Tarot/Oracle Cards

Essential Oils

Herbs

Feather

House Plants

Moon Dish

This lovely project requires air-dry clay to make a long curved-edged dish to sit your cleansing wand in, after use. It will be so precious that you'll want to display it on your altar all year.

Air-dry clay (Earth element) is a must for every crafty witch; it's affordable, easy to source and you can create some magical little projects that will make your home feel more unique. If you're wanting to do an activity during the full moon, this would be perfect, especially under an Earth sign, such as Taurus, Virgo or Capricorn.

I've used air-dry clay for years and have loved it ever since I was a young girl. During the summer holidays, I would sit outside at the garden table and roll clay beads for hours or make tiny plates. They would dry quickly in the sun and I would paint them the next day.

WHAT YOU'LL NEED:

* A wipeable mat to protect your table or surface

* 1 packet of air-dry clay (white)

* A little knife for cutting

* Rolling pin, but you can also use an empty bottle

* Acrylic paints (for this activity I used black, gold and base layer white)

* Paint brushes, 1 flat bristle and a thinner one for detail

* Soft cloth

* Sandpaper (optional)

* Acrylic varnish

PROCESS:

1. Wash your hands and prepare your surface for the mat and then the clay.
2. Cut off a small golf-ball-sized piece of clay and reseal the clay in the packet, so that it doesn't dry out whilst you're working.
3. Roll the clay between your hands to add flexibility and heat to it. If it's too dry, splash it with a little water.
4. Begin to roll using your rolling pin and flip it over occasionally so the clay spreads evenly. Roll until the clay is roughly 1 cm (½ in) thick.
5. If you need more clay, add more in now and repeat step 4.
6. Now you are going to create a rectangle shape but with curved edges. Think about your cleansing wand lying comfortably on the dish. The dish needs to be long enough to support the wand. Mine measures approximately 6 x 13 cm (2½ x 5 in). You can cut a rough shape and begin moulding the edges upwards to create a little rim.
7. This is going to have a beautiful irregular edge that will give it that organic look, so remember to have fun and don't try to make it look too perfect.
8. Once you're happy with the shape, allow it to dry for 24 hours.
9. Give your dry clay dish a gentle wipe over with a soft cloth to remove any

residue. If you want smoother edges, then use a little fine-grade sandpaper.
10. You can now paint three little moons. Use the black paint to represent the moon's shadow and gold paint to represent the moon's glow.
11. Now with a thinner brush, add the gold to the rim of the dish.
12. Now add two layers of varnish, allowing the first layer to dry before applying the next.

NIGHT

Night-time often heralds 'magic'. It typically signifies the end of the doing hours (conscious realm) and the beginning of the resting, restorative hours (subconscious realm).

Making time for simple magic is essential for realising what's important in life. In this final chapter, I've selected some beautiful crafting and self-care rituals that will nurture your mind, body and soul.

Some evenings will hold a certain type of magic; there may be a full moon or an ethereal glow to the sky, and you might feel eager to write in your journal or do a tarot or oracle reading. Other times, you'll just want to sit quietly and do nothing much at all.

Sometimes, making secret magical plans for a special evening can bring you focus and something to look forward to.

ANIMAL MEANINGS

Here are 21 animals and their spiritual meanings. Have any of them showed up in your dreams, or in your life, recently? Look out for animals that cross your path or show up for you in the form of art, jewellery, divination tools, oracle decks etc.

When you see these animals or a symbol of them, these are their messages to you.

BEAR - You are strong, connected to the earth and your determination will overcome challenges.

BEE - You are communicative, industrious, adaptable and lucky.

CAT - You are magical, mysterious, independent and creative.

FOX - You are intelligent, observant, committed and adaptable.

OWL - You are intuitive, attuned to your surroundings, intelligent and resilient.

CROW - You have strong psychic abilities, are strong willed and flexible.

SQUIRREL - You're playful, prudent, organised and efficient.

FROG - You are humble, patient and wise. You are blessed with good fortune.

HORSE - You are compassionate, spiritual, sensitive and affable.

BUTTERFLY - You are graceful, adaptable, clever and expressive.

DOG - You are loyal, responsible, dedicated and warm hearted.

SHEEP - You are humble, grounded, courageous and compassionate.

DRAGONFLY - You are wise beyond your years, free spirited and lucky.

MOTH - You are intuitive, generous, trustworthy and optimistic.

WHALE - You are communicative, spiritual, wise and loving.

HEDGEHOG - You are nurturing, relaxed, charming and gentle.

BADGER - You are determined, committed, confident and action orientated.

SWAN - You are faithful, adaptable, devoted and a visionary.

WOLF - You are self-confident, instinctive, intelligent and disciplined.

OTTER - You are curious, flexible, cheerful and cooperative.

DEER - You are strong, yet sensitive, gentle and tender.

New and Full Moon Bath Salts

Moon baths are a chance for you to invite magic into your home. It's a very special experience to light candles, fill your bath with a homemade potion and know that this time is entirely for you. It's not just self-care, it's soul-care. You are not only working with the elements of water and fire (using the flame of the candles), but you are creating a moment, perfectly timed with the moon, to relax and tap into your infinite creativity.

I used to house-sit for a woman who lived in a 400-year-old thatched cottage with the most exquisite rose garden. As the roses began to drop their petals, I would gather them all up and place them on trays to dry in the sun. The darker the petals, the more vivid the colour would be as they dried. I would also collect huge bundles of French lavender for drying.

I was thinking specifically about creating moon bath salts with the roses, which represent beauty and abundance. I dried handfuls of petals so I could use them as part of a full and new moon bath ritual and save extra for later projects.

This whole process was divinely magical to me, mainly because I was making the moon salts from scratch and with loving intention. Here, I share with you an easy, non-fancy yet super-magical moon bath salts recipe that I personally use.

WHAT YOU'LL NEED:

* 100 g (3½ oz) Epsom salts/pink Himalayan salt
* 2 tbsp dried lavender
* 2 tbsp dried rose petals
* Mortar and pestle (or electric food blender)
* Glass jar with lid
* 5 drops rose essential oil
* 5 drops lavender essential oil

Note: Essential oils are strong, so always follow instructions for use.

PROCESS:

Place the salts and dried flowers in a mortar and pestle. This is so you can grind the ingredients down to a finer consistency. Using the mortar and pestle is a slower and more traditional process than using a conventional blender, but a blender can be used.

When the salts and petals have ground down to a finer consistency, tip the mixture into a glass jar. Now you may add your essential oils. With a spoon, gently stir and fold the mixture, to ensure the oils are evenly distributed.

MOON SHOWER SACHETS:

IF YOU DON'T HAVE ACCESS TO A BATH, YOU CAN CREATE MOON SHOWER SACHETS. STILL MAKE THE EXPERIENCE SPECIAL BY ADDING PLANTS, CRYSTALS AND CANDLES IF YOU WISH, AND THEN FILL A COTTON/MUSLIN SQUARE WITH THE HERBS AND FLOWERS IN THE MOON BATH SALTS RECIPE ABOVE. RUN THE WATER OVER THE BAG TO RELEASE THE AROMAS.

If you are using large flower heads as part of your moon bath ritual, you can use a small net or strainer to capture the petals at the end of your bath.

For the full moon bath salts: add more flowers and scent of rose and lavender. This amplifies abundance and the ability to manifest. Flowers naturally evoke a feeling of beauty, expression and celebration, which is also strongly associated with the full moon.

For the new moon focus on muscle-soaking salts, to initiate deep relaxation. As your muscles relax during a new moon bath ritual, it releases stagnant energy from the body and allows clearer breathing.

For both recipes, add a handful or two of the moon bath salts to running water and swirl around clockwise with your hand to release the aromas.

You can add 1 tablespoon of dried eucalyptus, 1 tablespoon of rosemary or 1 tablespoon of mint. I also like to add a teaspoon of dried pine needles. Add 5–10 drops of your choice of essential oil.

COLOURFUL CANDLE MAGIC

Every witch loves candles. They play a primary role in conducting spells and rituals because they are a symbol of initiation. A candle represents the element of fire, and paired with a particular colour can help you focus on magical work, such as healing, manifesting, problem solving, cleansing or simply to create a specific mood.

Candles come in a plethora of colours and scents and are easy to source. You can use coloured tea-lights as well.

Use these pages to help you reference the colours and their meanings for the next time you conduct a spell or perhaps when you're planning a moon bath or dressing your altar to reflect the season.

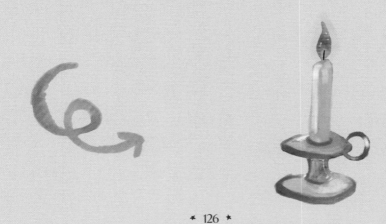

Red

Is used to harness power, inspire action, increase momentum towards starting projects and for creating romantic love spells based on a deep spiritual connection, as opposed to lust.

Pink

Pink candles represent a gentler energy, one that can inspire the feelings of unconditional love, friendship and sensual femininity.

Blue

Very pale blue is the colour that emulates a sense of peace and tranquillity, which is ideal when you want to create a space to meditate in, or during a soothing bath.

Yellow

The colour of the sun, representing the conscious mind and your awareness. Use a yellow candle during a solar eclipse, but also during rituals where you are seeking assistance with memory, study or tasks that require a more logical approach.

Purple

Is associated with royalty and authority. You can use a purple candle to empower yourself and enhance your psychic abilities.

Green

The colour instinctively linked to growth, burgeoning ideas and creativity. Green candles are perfect when conducting spells and rituals with the intention to heal or regenerate.

Orange

Is a friendly ally and can be used to comfort, inspire and bring clarity to you if you are feeling overwhelmed. Light an orange candle to invite in creativity and the feeling of having a big warm hug.

White

Represents the moon, but also denotes innocence, purity and clarity. It's ideal to light white candles to create protection rituals for your home. White gives an elegance and sense of magic to any room.

Black

This is a colour to be used wisely during banishing spells, but it also can be used during the waning and new moon, because it represents the absence of light. It is a fantastic colour to use when you want to release negative thought patterns, or if you're feeling unwell and need to shake off the energy. Black will absorb negative energy, so just make sure that you cleanse your space, before and after a ritual/spell.

Brown

Brings you down to Earth and can inspire feelings of being secure, stable and in control. It's perfect to use this colour candle paired with orange and white for a house blessing.

Moon Water

Moon water can be dabbed onto pulse points, which are where blood runs closest to the surface of the skin, such as your wrists, behind your ears and your temples.

Moon water can also be used to cleanse your home and the objects in it. Personally, I tend to use moon water to water my plants, and I often sprinkle it around my front door, for extra protection and good vibes.

Moon water has been used by practising witches for centuries because of its magical associations with love, abundance and harnessing the power to manifest.

You don't need to make moon water during an eclipse. Eclipses are associated with what's hidden; the focus is more on releasing what no longer serves and less about amplifying and celebrating.

Moon water is a favourite of mine to create. I've been sharing my process with my audience for years. Timing is a large element of creating moon-infused sacred water, but more importantly, it's the intention you hold in your body and how you programme the water that will give you the best results.

The moon represents the subconscious mind and the water signifies realms of emotions that are unseen or hidden. Creating moon water on a regular basis offers a magical opportunity to deepen your relationship with the moon, and to use the element of water and your subconscious mind to bring about abundance and joy in your waking life.

WHAT YOU'LL NEED:

* A clear head and calm disposition
* Glass, silver or ceramic vessel. I use a glass bottle with a natural cork lid.
* A clear crystal. Clear crystals hold a purer power and are perfect to charge with the light of a full moon. Charging a crystal means that the crystal is either cleansed and reset from previous use, or that its power is amplified.
* A quartz wand (optional)

PROCESS:

When dealing with the water that will be charged by the moon, it's preferable that you are barefoot and your hands and feet have been washed. Collect water from a natural water source, where the water is *living*. Rainwater collection is also fine. If you cannot find natural water, then filtered or distilled will do.

On the first light of a waxing moon, begin to add water to your bottle. Add in small increments as the moon waxes. There are approximately 11 days from the waxing moon to the full moon.

Place your moon water outside, ideally on granite/stone or natural material and as high up as possible.

Bring the moon water back inside during the day. Repeat this process until the full moon. Wash your hands and feet and sit with the water vessel in your hands. Try to be present. If you don't know what to say, or don't have a definite intention, all you need to do is to sit with the water and the moon. This is powerful and if you do this regularly, insights about the nature of your reality will come flooding in.

You can add the moon water to a little spray bottle with herbs/essential oils for a harmonious room mist or dab on your temples, chest, tummy and wrists to amplify good health, wealth and abundance.

COLOURING
ACTIVITY

WHAT MAKES ME FEEL COSY AND SAFE?

GUIDED MEDITATION

It's important that you carve time out for yourself during the new moon, to focus on how you want this next lunar phase to feel like...

And what it is you want to attract into your life.

. . . .

Begin by cleansing your entire aura, which is the energetic field that surrounds your body, starting with the top of your head.

Imagine a wave of warm, golden light gently touching your head and moving down through your neck, shoulder and chest.

It feels like a warm hug.

As the wave of golden light travels down through your heart, stomach, hips, thighs, knees and past your feet, you feel unburdened and your thoughts are clear and free of limiting thoughts.

Take a deep breath in and hold for three seconds, 1...2...3
Release and focus on all the air being pushed out from your lungs.
Now breath in fresh new moon energy, 1...2...3

View your body and ready yourself for this next lunar cycle, ready to step into an enhanced version of yourself.

Visualise being in an ancient woodland.
It's dusk and the sky is gently dimming.

One by one your favourite stars and constellations begin to appear like friends joining a gathering.

The ground is soft and mossy and you walk barefoot through to a glade that is surrounded by ancient oak and holly trees.

In the centre a crackling fire awaits you. You then sit comfortably by the fire. Imagine gentle music playing.

You stare into the fire.

You visualise your creative dreams.

You see the flames dance.

You feel the passion towards the ideas you have.
You ask for the motivation and sparks of energy needed to begin new projects or to initiate new habits.

You pick up a woodland wand and hold it in your hand.
The flames lick the air and reach up to the stars.

Circle your wand clockwise in front of the flames three times to bring about magnetic abundance.

Let go with your outward breath.

Take three more intentional breaths in and out to end this meditation.

New Moon Journal

Every year, I make an A5-sized notebook specifically for recording my new moon goals. I record my intentions and goals in my new moon journal as powerful affirmations, as if the wish has already been fulfilled.

I truly believe that if you can start to record regularly in a journal such as this, you can create profound changes in your life. For example, I recorded in my new moon journal several years ago that I would create my first book and work with an amazing publisher. I was so vivid in my belief that this was going to occur that, in that moment under a new moon, I knew what it would feel like to have such a dream come true. It was beautiful to find my new moon journal and reread some of the intentions I had — so many of them had come to fruition.

TIP: YOU CAN CREATE A MINI VISION BOARD AT THE FRONT OF EACH JOURNAL, OR DO A MINI JOURNAL SPREAD FOR EACH NEW MOON. TAKE PICTURES OUT OF MAGAZINES THAT INSPIRE YOU TO REACH A CERTAIN GOAL OR PRINT FROM THE INTERNET. YOU ARE AIMING TO CREATE A VISUAL TOOL THAT YOU CAN REFER TO WHEN YOU NEED A REMINDER OF WHERE YOUR FOCUS SHOULD GO.

Focus on eliminating old thought patterns that have been holding you back. See this time as a fresh start, and with it a renewed energy that will help you solidify what you want and where you want to be heading. I've included zodiac influences for the new moon to give you further ideas of what to focus on. Every two or three days, the moon will move through a different zodiac sign.

For example: When you are making plans for the new lunar cycle under the new moon, you may consider the current astrological sign. So, if the new moon is in Aries, you can use the fiery influence to kickstart a project.

WHAT YOU'LL NEED:

* Standard A4 white paper
* Waxed thread or embroidery thread
* Strong needle
* Scissors
* Paper clips
* A thick darning needle to make the holes

In your journal you might write:

New moon in Aries (and the date)

I am funnelling my energy into...

I will use this Aries energy to kickstart...

My three main goals during this next lunar cycle are...

PROCESS:

1

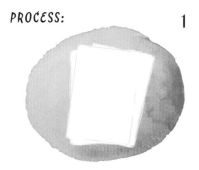

Begin with 10 separate pieces of paper (I cut five A4 sheets in half for a smaller journal). Gather them up and fold them in half.

2

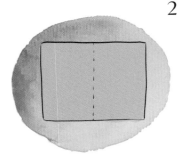

Open the folded paper and clamp it on both sides, so it doesn't move during sewing. Mark out holes with a ruler down the centrefold. Use the darning needle to make the holes. Five holes will do.

3

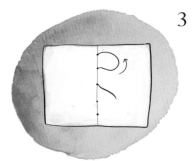

Thread your needle, but don't knot the end. Start from the inside middle hole, pull thread through the outside, leaving a 5 cm (2 in) of thread on the inside (you'll need this later)

4

Holding the pages landscape, sew to the right of your journal first, then back to the centre, then repeat on the left.

5

Once you've done this, sew back towards the centre hole that you started with. Turn the journal from front to back as you work, so it's easier to see the stitches.

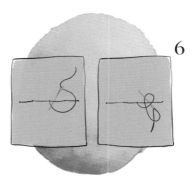

6

On the last stitch, sew to the outside and tie a knot (don't cut thread yet). Now thread through to the inside where your length of cord remains. Gently pull the thread end through the pages and tie it with the inside cord. Tuck ends in and cut.

7

Fold inside papers together and the cover in the opposite direction. Then fold the front cover back and clamp the entire journal together or use a weight (such as a few heavy books)

8

Leave for a day and now you can decorate the front by drawing or painting a 'New Moon Journal' and adding magical foliage.

WHEN THE NEW MOON IS IN ARIES:

Utilise the practical and enthusiastic mood to focus on short bursts of energy that make waves, invite fresh new energy into your home or begin a new project.

WHEN THE NEW MOON IS IN CANCER:

It's time to nurture yourself at a deeper level; when you let yourself be vulnerable, you'll actually become more confident and accepting of yourself. Water the seeds of your garden well – and those of your dreams. Nourish, nourish, nourish.

WHEN THE NEW MOON IS IN LEO:

Use your big, beautiful heart to pulse out loving and courageous energy into the ether. Recognise your wonderful qualities and talents, and funnel energy and loving light into projects you have in mind.

WHEN THE NEW MOON IS IN LIBRA:

Your mood may shift into areas of relationships. The heightened sense of beauty, balance and aesthetics plays a part in how you'll shape your new moon goals.

WHEN THE NEW MOON IS IN CAPRICORN:

Take responsibility and be the leader of your own life. Rituals and rhythms will assist you in strengthening your mindset. Harness Capricorn's determination and ambition to focus on the goals you want to achieve.

WHEN THE NEW MOON IS IN AQUARIUS:

Focus on collaboration, communication and experimenting with new ideas or solutions. Your energy has the ability to positively impact those around you. Taking a philosophical approach to life will help you overcome any challenges.

WHEN THE NEW MOON IS IN TAURUS:

Centre and ground yourself, let go of any stubbornness or ego that's holding you back from certain projects. Relax. The Taurus energy is full of resourcefulness, so use this as you plan for the next lunar cycle. Planting physical seeds under this new moon is extraordinarily powerful.

WHEN THE NEW MOON IS IN GEMINI:

This is the time to harmonise growth and restrict growth, like a gardener looking for the very best way to prune and care for their plants. This is your time for gathering ideas, researching, reaching out and communicating in a fun and affable way.

WHEN THE NEW MOON IS IN VIRGO:

Your mood may encourage you to look at more practical and analytical tasks. Use the new moon to organise, sort, delegate and honour your body and home. Planning and goal-setting will be powerful during this time.

WHEN THE NEW MOON IS IN SCORPIO:

Step back from the noise and trivialities of gossip and go inward. Dip into the metaphysical and mystical realms by spending quiet moments alone and in nature. Do a social media cleanse, cut back on your to-do list, and use this time to encourage new growth for burgeoning ideas.

WHEN THE NEW MOON IS IN SAGITTARIUS:

Use the optimistic and nature-loving influence to get outside and be with nature. Give your ideas room to grow and create a beautiful space to meditate or relax in. Rewild yourself. Nourish your wanderlust.

WHEN THE NEW MOON IS IN PISCES:

The full moon is powerful in Pisces; the new moon is more subtle and less sensitive, but still it's an opportunity to get more intimate with your desires. Your imagination and sensitivity will assist you in creating some seriously magical goals.

Sleep-Well Fragrant Pillow

When I think of this crafting activity, I always think of my grandmother. She would hang up miniature hand-embroidered linen pillows filled with lavender in her wardrobe to keep her clothes fresh and the moths away, but she also had similar ones near the guest beds. Since then, I've made many for myself and for my daughters, with the intention that they bring about a restful night's sleep.

Lavender is the go-to aromatic plant for anything associated with relaxation and sleep. It has antibacterial properties and is also known for its calming effect. It is easy to source, but you can also grow it yourself.

For a secret boost of magic, this little pillow will have a spell infused within it.

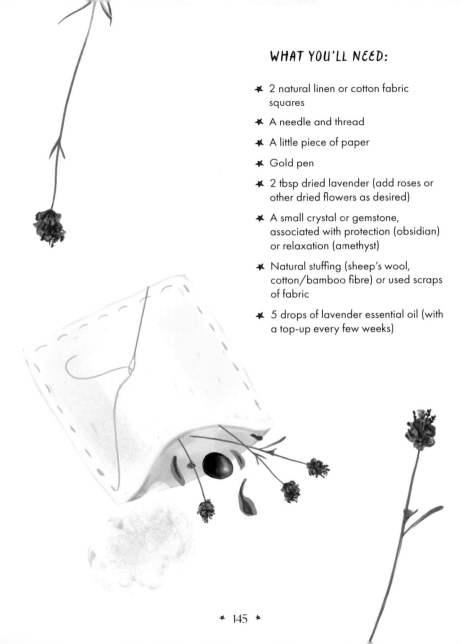

WHAT YOU'LL NEED:

- ✦ 2 natural linen or cotton fabric squares
- ✦ A needle and thread
- ✦ A little piece of paper
- ✦ Gold pen
- ✦ 2 tbsp dried lavender (add roses or other dried flowers as desired)
- ✦ A small crystal or gemstone, associated with protection (obsidian) or relaxation (amethyst)
- ✦ Natural stuffing (sheep's wool, cotton/bamboo fibre) or used scraps of fabric
- ✦ 5 drops of lavender essential oil (with a top-up every few weeks)

PROCESS:

1

You don't need to be a whizz at sewing for this project, it's nice and simple. Place the front sides of your two fabric squares together (facing each other) and sew around the edges, leaving a 5 mm (¼ in) seam allowance. Make sure you leave a 2.5 cm (1 in) gap, so you can turn the pillow the right side out.

2

Now for the spell. Spells should be carefully considered, so pick an intention for this pillow. What does it represent? What is its purpose? What energy do you want it to hold?

3

With a gold pen, write a spell that infuses the idea of healthy, uninterrupted sleep for regeneration, restoration and healing. You may want to set the intention that this pillow helps you to dream more lucidly and profoundly. You could also include a sigil on the paper.

4

Once you've written your spell, roll it up and place it inside the pillow. Add the dried lavender, the crystal and the stuffing, then sew up the hole.

5

Add a few drops of essential oil onto the fabric and tuck it under your pillow.

You can make a 'worries be gone' pillow, which is similar to a worry doll. You could also make a few different variations, using different spells, colours, flowers and oils.

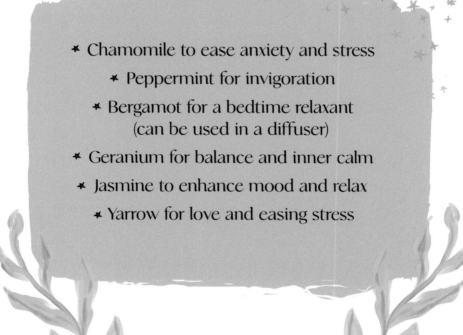

* Chamomile to ease anxiety and stress
* Peppermint for invigoration
* Bergamot for a bedtime relaxant (can be used in a diffuser)
* Geranium for balance and inner calm
* Jasmine to enhance mood and relax
* Yarrow for love and easing stress

MOON RITUALS

Over the years, I've been deepening my connection to the moon and the rituals I use to enhance my spiritual journey. Rituals are a sacred time for you to focus on an intention and to connect with the divine feminine energy of the moon.

Rituals also empower you to move forward with projects, gain spiritual insights and to release negative thoughts.

There are eight main phases that represent the entire lunar cycle and each one has its own unique energy and purpose. Humans have used the moon to time farming and home activities for centuries. The moon is essentially a timer and each full moon has a name associated with the seasonal appearance of flowers or animals.

I've created eight rituals to represent each moon phase. It's not necessary to do every single one in a lunar cycle; trust the timing of things and choose a ritual that aligns with the moon and your activities.

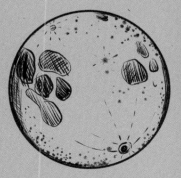

NEW MOON

 ### SACRED INTENTION RITUAL

Cleanse yourself and space with smoking sage. Light a black candle under the new moon. You are now inviting in the energy of new ideas, fresh starts and resetting the energy.

Whilst the candle is burning, make a dark drink (tea is preferable). Wait patiently for it to brew, pour into a cup and visualise the abundance and new ideas pouring into your life.

Stir anticlockwise for protection moving forward.

Write intentions and plans on separate pieces of paper and place in a jar with a quartz crystal.

Depending on the season, now is the perfect moment to plant a bulb or seeds.

WAXING CRESCENT

 MOON WATER RITUAL

As the moon reveals her first silvery crescent as a young moon, it's the perfect time to begin making moon water.

Fill the jar quarter full and place a quartz crystal inside. Secure the lid. Hold in your hands for a while and call on the moon to infuse the water with power, abundance and protection. Place on a mirror for extra magical power.

Bring in each night and top up as the moon continues to wax. After the full moon, bring in your jar and add to a spray bottle for plants and to bless your home or anoint your body.

WAXING HALF MOON

 ### MOON MAIDEN RITUAL

Amplify love, youthfulness and connection to the Maiden Goddess of the Moon. Light a pink candle and use pink quartz.

Take a silver or clear dish and fill with water. Stir with a quartz point to activate the water. Now add a drop of rose or lavender essential oil. You can place a small flower in the dish too.

Place the dish outside or on a windowsill and focus on the vibration of love. Ask for the Maiden Goddess to bring you continued health, inner beauty and youthfulness.

WAXING GIBBOUS

 COURAGE RITUAL USING THE ELEMENT OF FIRE

If you are seeking courage at this time, create a simple fire ritual to invoke passion, bravery and inspiration.

Gather a collection of spices such as star anise, cinnamon and chilli flakes.

Make an invigorating tea (chai or similar).
Sit quietly with your tea, hold your crystal in your hands and think of where you need the most strength in your life.

Write it down on a piece of paper and fold three times.
Place your crystal on top of the paper until you've finished your tea.
Hold once more, before letting go and burning in your heatproof dish. Add a pinch of spices to it and light a candle.

Call on St Brigid the Goddess of Metalwork, Midwifery, Poetry and Creativity, to bless your home and embolden you with courage.

FULL MOON

 ### MAGICAL MANIFESTATION RITUAL

Call on the five sacred elements, Earth (North), Air (East), Fire (South), Water (West) and Spirit (Centre) into your full moon ritual. Light five candles.

Write down your wishes for the future and act as if they have already been fulfilled. Thank the Goddess of the Moon for her powerful energy and to bless future projects.

Soak up the magic and amplify beauty and emotional insights by adding moon water to your bath. Add rose petals, rose/lavender essential oil and Epsom salts.

Make a full moon cake to celebrate your successes and abundance, drink wine and get luxurious!

WANING GIBBOUS

 ### SACRED RELEASE RITUAL

During the full moon and as the moon wanes, it's the ideal time to reflect on lessons learnt and to release preconceptions and limitations that you've placed on yourself or that others have.

In order to heal, you must cleanse first.

Identify what you wish to let go of on a piece of paper and fold three times.

In your heatproof dish, place a small handful of Epsom salts and throw in a sprig of rosemary for protection.

As you throw in the paper and light, visualise the burden being lifted and your worries vaporising with the smoke.

Repeat as necessary. Play music, make it special and prepare a sleepy time tea for a good night's sleep.

$\mathcal{W}$ANING $\mathcal{H}$ALF $\mathcal{M}$OON

 MOON LOVER RITUAL

This part of the lunar cycle signifies the beginning of self-care time, so a love ritual is perfect.

Create a nature mandala with the crystal at the centre. Add circles of petals and other objects that exude love. Write a love note to yourself or someone else. You can write in a pink pen.

Place your moon water on your altar and anoint your note with a dab then place under your crystal.

In your right hand place a pink quartz and in your left a clear quartz. Now you will focus on the vibration of love and sending your love out into the Universe and to all living beings.

Thank the Goddess of the Moon
for her emotional guidance.

Leave on your altar for three days.